C0-APZ-256

HAWAII

PHOTOGRAPHY BY GREG LAWSON   ENGLISH • ESPAÑOL • FRANÇAIS • DEUTSCH • 日本語

Published in the United States by

First Choice

P.O. Box 23001
Santa Barbara, California 93121

© Copyright 1985 and 1986 by First Choice Publishers. All rights reserved.
Library of Congress Catalog Card Number 83-81363
HAWAII ISBN 0-916251-25-X

PHOTOGRAPHY / GREG LAWSON
INTRODUCTION / TINA GOOLSBY
CAPTIONS / DAVID MICHAELS
BOTANICAL CAPTIONS / MARY SHELDON
TRANSLATIONS / GAVIN HYDE, SUZANNE LAFOND
ROSELINDE KONRAD, KIMIE SMITH
TYPOGRAPHY / FRIEDRICH TYPOGRAPHY
PRINTING / DAI NIPPON PRINTING CO. JAPAN

Our titles currently available or in production include: ARIZONA, CALIFORNIA, COLORADO,
HAWAII, LOS ANGELES, SAN DIEGO, SAN FRANCISCO, SANTA BARBARA, WESTERN OREGON.

HAWAII

Eons ago, Hawaii emerged from the ocean depths. Molten lava erupted from volcanoes to build mountainous islands. Today it is a cornucopia of nature, culture, and contrast whose fruits are scattered over a small area of the North Pacific. It is literally (and otherwise) a steppingstone linking East to West. Here Polynesian sensuality, American pragmatism, and Oriental exoticism weave a tapestry of cultural extremes.

According to one legend, *The Big Island* was first discovered by Hawaii-loa, who bumped into it while sailing towards the planet Jupiter in a sea shell. Anthropologists tell us that the first Polynesians came to the Islands some twelve to fifteen hundred years ago, searching the seas as we search outer space today. These early settlers brought the life sustaining plants of sugar cane, bananas, coconuts, yams, taro and breadfruit. Their culture included music, dance and sacred ceremony.

The remote Hawaiian Islands were one of the last places to be discovered by western explorers. British Captain James Cook came upon them in 1778. Forty years later, by dint of American missionary influence, they became a primary source of sugar cane and pineapples for a world market. Labor was imported first from China, then Portugal, Japan, and the Phillipines. Today Hawaii is a true ethnic melting pot with a multitude of possible racial/national blends.

Its temperate climate, warm surrounding waters, and palm-studded beaches lure millions of visitors each year. Present too are dramatic volcanoes and varied bouquets of a thousand flowers. Though only a speck in the giant Pacific, each of the islands has its own special allure. Consider the populated islands from southeast to northwest. Two live volcanoes, *paniolos* and cattle ranches, an altitude range of nearly fourteen thousand feet, and Hilo (the southernmost city in the States) are just part of what make *The Big Island*, **Hawaii**, a land of startling contrasts. Across the Alenuihaha Channel lies *The Valley Island*, **Maui**, a cosmopolitan isle with thirty three miles of heavenly beachfront, glamourous sun splashed resorts, lush valleys and "The House of the Sun"—Haleakala. **Lanai**, *The Pineapple Island*, is for the most part privately owned by Castle & Cook, Inc., parent to Dole Pineapple. Across the water from the reef-shrouded north coast of Lanai is **Molokai**, *The Friendly Island*, so named for the amicability of its native inhabitants. Its western neighbor, **Ohau**, *The Gathering Place* holds eighty percent of Hawaii's residents, most of whom live in Honolulu. **Kauai**, *The Garden Isle*, claims the wettest spot on earth as well as a barren desert within its boundries, and brims with beauty in between. Next is **Niihau**, a privately owned cattle and sheep ranch, employing nearly all the two hundred pureblood Hawaiians who live there.

To experience all that is Hawaii is to take an excursion into paradise. The beauty and variety of these islands, as represented by the following photographs, offer themselves to everyone who comes ashore. And the spirit of Aloha is sure to linger, like the scent of the fragrant plumeria lei, long after your departure.

HAWAII

Hace eones, Hawaii nació de las profundidades del océano. Lava fundida brotó de volcanes para formar islas montañosas. Hoy es cornucopia de la naturaleza y fuente de cultura cuyos frutos están desparramados sobre una zona diminutiva del Pacífico norteño. Es literalmente (y en abstracción) el estriberón entre Oriente y Occidente. Aquí la sensualidad polinesia, el pragmatismo americano y el exotismo oriental forjan un tejido de extremos culturales.

Según cierta leyenda, *La Isla Grande* fue descubierta primero por Hawaii-Loa, quien chocó con ella navegando su concha velera hacia la planeta Júpiter. Los antropólogos nos informan que los primeros polinesios vinieron a las islas hace entre mil doscientos y mil quinientos años, explorando el mar como exploramos hoy el espacio. Estos primeros colonizadores trajeron plantas alimentosas como la caña de azúcar, bananos, cocos, ñames, taro, y árboles de pan. Su cultura incluía música, danza, y rito sagrado.

Las remotas Islas de Hawaii figuran entre los últimos lugares visitados por exploradores europeos. El capitán inglés James Cook los encontró en el año 1778. Cuarenta años más tarde, como resultado de la influencia de misioneros americanos, llegaron a ser la fuente principal de la caña de azúcar y piñas para un mercado mundial. Primero trajeron obreros de la China, después desde Portugal, el Japón y de las Islas Filipinas. Hoy Hawaii es un verdadero crisol étnico con una variedad espléndida de mezclas de sangres y nacionalidades.

Su clima moderada, aguas templadas, y playas adornadas de palmeras atraen a millones de turistas cada año. Destacan también los volcanes dramáticos y multitudes de ramos de flores de muchas especies. No siendo más que granos en la tremenda extensión del Pacífico, cada isla tiene su imán particular. Revisando las islas pobladas, empezando en el sureste y procediendo hacia el noroeste: dos volcanes activos, *paniolos* y ranchos ganaderos, sierras que llegan a casi 4300 metros, e Hilo (la ciudad mas al sur de las de los EE.UU.) comprenden solo una parte de los que da a la *Isla Grande*, **Hawaii**, su aspecto de tierra de contrastes chocantes. Cruzando el canal de Alenuihaha llegamos a la *Isla de Valles*, **Maui**, ínsula cosmopolita con cincuenta y tres kilómetros de playas paradisíacas, soleados balnearios encantadores, valles frondosos y *"La Casa del Sol"* — Haleakala. **Lanai**, la *Isla de Piñas*, es principalmente propiedad de la compañía Castle & Cook, firma fundadora de Dole Pineapple. Saltando otro estrecho de agua, y frente a la costa norteña, llena de arrecifes, de Lanai — está **Molokai**, la *isla Amistosa*, así denominada por la simpatía de sus habitantes indígenas. Su vecina hacia el oeste, **Oahu**, *Sitio de Reunión*, es el hogar del ochenta por ciento de los residentes de Hawaii, la mayoría de ellos viviendo en Honolulu. **Kauai**, la *Isla Frondosa*, se jacta del sitio más lluvioso del mundo y sin embargo puede ostentar un desierto estéril en su geografía. Entre tales polos todo es hermosura. Después viene **Niihau**, de propiedad privada, utilizada como rancho ganadero donde encuentran empleo dos centenares de Hawaiianos de pura sangre que allí residen.

Experimentar todo lo que es Hawaii es someterse a una romería de vuelta al Paraíso. La hermosura y variedad de estas islas, que las fotografías aquí ofrecidas tratan de reflejar, hacen huésped al que desembarque. Y queda el encanto del espíritu de *Aloha* dentro del viajero, como el aroma del fragrante *plumeria lei*, mucho tiempo después de la partida.

HAWAII

Il y a déjà bien longtemps, Hawaii surgit des profondeurs de l'océan. Des éruptions volcaniques en se refroidissant ont formé des îles montagneuses. Aujourd'hui, Hawaii représente une corne d'abondance qui nous offre les charmes de la nature, une culture unique et mille contrastes tous réunis sur une étendue fort petite du Pacifique Nord. C'est vraiment un lien entre l'est et l'ouest. La sensualité polynésienne, le pragmatisme américain et l'exotisme oriental tissent une tapisserie de fils divers.

D'après une légende, *The Big Island* fut découverte par Hawaii-loa, qui s'y heurta en voguant vers Jupiter dans sa barque en coquillage. Les anthropologistes prétendent que les premiers polynésiens sont arrivés aux îles il y a douze à quinze cent ans à la recherche des océans comme le font de nos jours les astronautes avec leurs voyages interplanétaires. Les premiers colons apportèrent des plantes nourissantes telles que la canne à sucre, le bananier, la noix de coco, l'igname, le taro et le *breadfruit*. Leur expression culturel se manifesta dans la musique, la danse et les cérémonies sacrées.

Les îles hawaiiennes lointaines furent une des dernières découvertes des explorateurs de l'ouest. Le capitaine anglais James Cook les trouva en 1778. Quarante ans plus tard, à force d'influence de la part des missionaires américains, les îles devinrent une source primaire de la canne à sucre et d'ananas au marché mondial. La main d'œuvre vint d'abord de la Chine, ensuite du Portugal, du Japon et des Phillipines. Aujourd'hui on trouve à Hawaii un mélange et une fusion de races et d'éléments ethniques de toutes sortes.

Son climat tempéré, les eaux chaudes qui entourent les îles, les palmiers qui ornent les plages attirent des foules de voyageurs chaque année. On y trouve aussi des volcans dramatiques et des bouquets garnis de mille fleurs. A peine une tache sur le Pacifique géant, chacune des îles a une allure, un charme spécial. Remarquez par exemple les îles peuplées du sud-est allant vers le nord-ouest. Vous y trouverez deux volcans, les *paniolos* et des ranch où on fait l'élevage de bestiaux, des montagnes dont l'altitude s'élève jusqu'à 4000 mètres, et Hilo (la ville la plus au sud de toute autre dans les Etats Unis) tout cela ne sont que quelques exemples des contrastes étonnant que l'on trouve à *The Big Island*, **Hawaii**. De l'autre coté du canal Alenuihaha se trouve *The Valley Island* **Maui**, une île cosmopolite qui a 50 kilomètres de plage, de superbes stations balnéaires, des vallées luxuriantes et "La Maison du Soleil" — Haleakala. **Lanai**, *The Pineapple Island*, est en partie une île privée, appartenant à Castle & Cook, Inc., Une société liée à Dole Pineapple. **Molokai**, *The Friendly Island*, ainsi nommée due à l'amabilité de ses habitants, se trouve de l'autre coté des récifs qui contournent la rive nord de Lanai. Ses voisins à l'ouest, **Oahu**, *The Gathering Place* compte quatre-vingt pourcent des habitants de Hawaii et la plupart de ceux-ci se trouvent à Honolulu. **Kauai**, *The Garden Isle*, se dit l'endroit le plus pluvieux au monde et en même temps ses frontières contiennent un désert infertile et malgré tout, elle est d'une beauté extraordinaire. Il y a ensuite **Niihau**, un ranch particulier ou on fait l'élevage du bétail, vaches et moutons et où on emploie presque tous les deux cents hawaiiens pur sang qui s'y trouvent.

Afin de connaitre tout ce que représente Hawaii, il faut faire une excursion au paradis. La beauté et la variété de ces îles telles que représentées dans les photographies qui suivent, sont offertes à tout ceux qui y débarquent. L'essence même de Aloha lanquira comme le parfum de plumeria lei, et suivra pendant longtemps ceux qui les auront connues.

HAWAII

Hawaii ist vor Äonen aus den Tiefen des Meeres hervorgegangen. Seine gebirgigen Inseln entstanden aus der flüssigen Lava vulkanischer Ausbrüche. Heute ist es geradezu ein Füllhorn der Natur, Kultur und der Gegensätze, dessen Früchte über einen kleinen Teil des nördlichen Pazifik verstreut sind. Es ist buchstäblich und in jeder Beziehung ein Verbindungsglied zwischen Ost und West, ist es doch der Ort, wo polynesische Sinnenfreude, amerikanischer Pragmatismus und orientalische Exotik in all ihrer Gegensätzlichkeit zu einem bunten Gewirk miteinander verwoben sind.

Einer alten Sage nach wurde *die große Insel* zufällig von Hawaii-loa entdeckt, als er in einer Seemuschel auf den Planeten Jupiter zusteuerte. Die Anthropologen berichten, daß die ersten Polynesier vor etwa zwölf- bis fünfzehnhundert Jahren auf die Inseln kamen, als sie die Meere erforschten, wie wir heute den Raum. Diese frühen Siedler brachten lebenswichtige Früchte mit sich, nämlich Zuckerrohr, Bananen, Kokosnüsse, Jam- und Zehrwurzeln wie auch Brotfrüchte. Musik, Tanz und religiöses Zeremoniell spielten eine Rolle in ihrer Kultur.

Die entlegenen Hawaiischen Inseln gehören zu den spätesten Entdeckungen westlicher Erforscher. Der britische Kapitän James Cook stieß im Jahre 1778 auf sie. Vierzig Jahre später wurden sie durch den fördernden Einfluß amerikanischer Missionstätigkeit zu einer Hauptquelle für Rohrzucker und Ananas auf dem Weltmarkt. Die Arbeitskräfte wurden zunächst aus China geholt, später aus Portugal, Japan und den Philippinen. Heute ist Hawaii ein regelrechter Schmelztiegel der verschiedenen Völker und Rassen.

Das gemäßigte Klima, die warme Meeresströmung und die palmbesetzten Strände locken jedes Jahr Millionen von Besuchern herbei. Typisch sind übrigens die gewaltigen Vulkane und die ungeheure bunte Blumenfülle. Obwohl diese Inseln nur winzige Flecken im riesigen Pazifik darstellen, hat jedoch jede von ihnen ihre eigene Anziehungskraft. Man denke an die dichtbevölkerten Inseln auf der Südost-Nordwest-Achse. Zwei tätige Vulkane, *Panielos* und große Güter mit Viehwirtschaft, eine Höhenlage von durchschnittlich 4000 m und außerdem Hilo, die südlichste Stadt der Vereinigten Staaten, sind nur ein Bruchteil dessen, was *der großen Insel*, **Hawaii**, ihre erstaunliche Mannigfaltigkeit verleiht. Jenseits des Alenuihaha-Kanals liegt *die Talinsel* Maui, eine modern entwickelte Insel mit einem 50 km langen herrlichen Strand, eleganten, sonnenbeschienenen Badeorten, mit üppigen Tälern und Haleakala, dem „Haus der Sonne". **Lanai**, *die Ananas-Insel*, ist zum größten Teil im Privatbesitz der Firma Castle & Cook, Inc., der Muttergesellschaft von Dole, der Ananasfirma. Der zerklüfteten Nordküste von Lanai gegenüber liegt **Molokai**, *die freundliche Insel*, so benannt nach der Aufgeschlossenheit ihrer einheimischen Bewohner. Ihr Nachbar nach Westen hin ist **Oahu**, *der Tummelplatz*, wo achtzig Prozent der Bewohner Hawaiis leben, die meisten davon in Honolulu. **Kauai**, *die Garteninsel*, kann sich innerhalb ihres Bereichs sowohl der feuchtesten Gegend der Welt rühmen, wie auch einer kahlen Wüste; neben diesen Extremen besitzt sie landschaftliche Schönheit im Übermaß. Als nächstes ist **Niihau** zu nennen, eine Vieh- und Schafzucht-Ranch in Privatbesitz, wo nahezu alle dort ansässigen vollblütigen Hawaiianer beschäftigt sind.

All das zu verstehen, was wir Hawaii nennen, heißt einen Ausflug ins Paradies machen. Die Schönheit und Vielfältigkeit dieser Inseln, wie sie in den folgenden Fotografien dargestellt ist, ist jedem zugänglich, der den Fuß auf ihren Boden setzt. Noch lange, nachdem man sie wieder verlassen hat, ist das Fluidum des „Aloha" zu spüren, wie der Duft der berühmten Blumengirlanden.

HAWAII

昔、昔、大昔のこと、ハワイは深海の底より出現しました。海底火山よりふき出た溶岩は、やがて山の多い緑の島々となりました。そして今日のハワイは、豊かな自然と種々の文化を織りなす対照あふれる土地となり、北太平洋の一角を占めるこの小さな島々に、その美事な文化の果実を結んでいます。

ハワイの伝説の一つによれば、「大島」と呼ばれるハワイ島は、貝殻の船に乗り木星（ジュピター）を目指して船出したハワイ・ロア神が偶然たどりついて見つけたのだそうです。人類学者は、最初のポリネシア人がハワイ諸島にやって来たのは約1200年から1500年程昔のことだといっています。丁度、今日の人間が宇宙の探険に出かけるように、彼等も太平洋の大海原（うなばら）に乗り出したのでしょう。これら初期の居住者達は、砂糖きび、バナナ、ココナッツ、カム芋、タロ芋、パンの樹といった、彼等の生活に欠くことの出来ない植物を運んで来ました。文化的な面では、音楽、踊り、宗教儀式といったものも持って来ました。

遠隔の地にあったために、西洋の探険家達がハワイを発見したのは、ずっと年代が下ってあらのことでした。イギリスのキャプテン・ジェームス・クックがやって来たのは1778年のことでした。。その40年後には、アメリカの宣教師達の力によって、ハワイはすでに、砂糖きび、パイナップルの世界市場における主要な供給地となっていました。農園の労働力は、最初は中国から、その後ポルトガル、日本、フィリピンから連れてこられました。今日のハワイは、ありとあらゆる人種と国籍が多様に溶け混った、真の人種の坩堝（るつぼ）となっています。

温暖な気候と回りをとり囲む温い海、そしてやしの葉のなびく浜辺は、年間何百万という旅行者達を魅了してやみません。雄大なる山々、四季咲き乱れる何千種類に及ぶ花の群。太平洋のただ中、ほんのけし粒程の大きさながら、島の一つ一つは、それぞれ違った魅力をもっています。東南から北西に列ぶ島々を御想像下さい。

二つの活火山、パニオロスと呼ばれるカーボーイと海抜1400フィートに及ぶ牧場、そしてアメリカ合衆国中最南端に位置するヒロ市。これらはハワイ島の持つ魅力のほんの一例にすぎません。ここからアレヌイハナ海峡をはさんだ対岸は「渓谷の島」といわれるマウイ島です。30マイルに及ぶ美しい砂浜、太陽の光あふれるリゾート地、緑豊かな渓谷は国際的に知られ、太陽の女神ハレアカラの住家ともいわれます。「パイナップルの島」ラナイ島は、ドール・パイナップル社の親会社であるキャッスル・クック社が島とほとんどを私有しています。珊瑚礁に囲まれたこのラナイ島の北方には、「友情の島」モロカイ島が横たわっています。これは人情味豊かなこの島の住民にちなんで名づけられた名前です。このモロカイ島の西方にはオアフ島があります。ハワイ州の人口80パーセントを占めるオアフ島は、ハワイ全島の「集会場」でもあり、そのほとんどの人口はホノルル市に集中しています。「庭園の島」カウアイ島には、世界一雨量の多いといわれる地点とともに荒涼とした砂漠地帯が共存し、その中間には絶妙なる緑豊かな自然の美が展開されています。最後はニイハウ島。ここは全島私有の牧場地で、200人程の純血のハワイ人達のほとんどが、そこで働いています。

ハワイの醍醐味を味うためには、是非一度この楽園を訪ずれなくてはなりません。以下写真集に紹介されている変化に富んだ美しさを御観賞下さい。プルメリアの花のレイの芳香が、島を離れた後も長く辺りに漂うように、友情の精神、アロハ・スピリットも長くあなたの心の中に残ることでしょう。

HAWAII

A single coconut rests on a spotless beach near Makahonu Point, windward Oahu.

Un coco solitario vino a parar en una playa inmaculada cerca de *Makahonu Point*, Oahu.

Seule, sur une plage immaculée, une noix de coco au vent de Oahu près de *Makahonu Point*.

Eine vereinzelte Kokusnuß liegt auf einem makellosen Strand in der Nähe von *Makahonu Point*, auf der Windseite von Oahu.

白砂にたたずむヤシの木。　オアフ島マカホヌ岬の近くにて。

Dainty impatiens cluster around an angular trunk deep in the forested Hana District of Maui.
(right) A gentle flow of Akaka Falls, north of Hilo.

Impatiens delicadas florecen alrededor de un tronco angular dentro del verdoso distrito de Hana en Maui.
(dcha.) La suave cascada de *Akaka Falls* al norte de Hilo.

Délicates impatientes forment un bouquet autour d'un tronc d'arbre à l'angle curieux, en pleine fôret dans le *Hana District* de Maui.   (à droite) Un écoulement paisible de la chute *Akaka Falls*, au nord de Hilo.

Mitten im bewaldeten Teil von Maui, dem Hana-Bezirk, wachsen Büschel von „fleißigen Lieschen" um einen schiefstehenden Baumstamm.   (rechts) Sanftes Gefälle der *Akaka Falls* nördlich von Hilo.

マウイ島ハナ地区。　森の奥深く咲き乱れる可憐なるインパチェンスの花の群。　（右）　アカカ滝。　ヒロ市の北。

August cliffs of Molokai's northeast Pali Coast are among the most spectacular in the Islands.
(left) Angels' Trumpet.

Los augustos precipicios de *Pali Coast* al noroeste de Molokai se cuentan entre los màs impresionantes
de las islas.   (izqda.) La flor Trompeta de Angel.

Falaises imposantes de Molokai nord-est de *Pali Coast* sont parmi les plus spectaculaires que l'on puisse trouver
dans les îles.   (à gauche) Trompette des anges.

Die erhabenen Felsen der nordöstlichen *Pali Coast* von Molokai gehören zu den eindrucksvollsten dieser Inseln.
(links) „Angels' Trumpet"

モロカイ島北岸パリコーストにそびえ立つ断崖は、ハワイ諸島中屈指の壮観です。   （左）　エンジェル・トランペットの花。

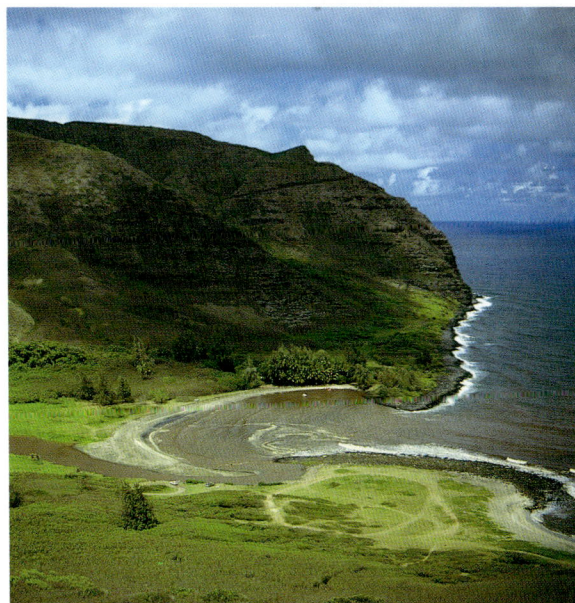

Hibiscus, the state flower. (right) Halawa Valley, Molokai. (left) A single peak in Oahu's Koolau Range backdrops native vegetation.

El *hibisco*, flor estatal de Hawaii. (dcha.) El valle de *Halawa*, Molokai. (izqda.) Un pico solitario de la sierra de *Koolau* en Oahu se alza sobre la vegetación.

Hibiscus, fleur emblématique de l'état. (à droite) La vallée *Halawa Valley*, Molokai. (à gauche) Une seule cime faisant partie des montagnes *Koolau Range* à Oahu, forme l'arrière plan à la végétation sauvage.

Hibiscus, das Blumensymbol des Staates Hawaii. (rechts) *Halawa Valley* auf Molokai. (links) Vereinzelter Berggipfel in der *Koolau Range* auf Oahu bildet den Hintergrund für die heimische Vegetation.

ハワイの州花、ハイビスカス。 （右） モロカイ島ハラワ渓谷。
（左） オアフ島コオラウ山脈の頂上と土着の植物。

A Hawaiian girl strolls Oahu's Kaaawa Beach Park.

Una hawaiana pasea en el parque *Kaaawa Beach* de Oahu.

Une jeune hawaiienne se promène dans le parc *Kaaawa Beach Park*, Oahu.

Eine Hawaiin wandert im *Kaaawa Beach Park* auf Oahu den Strand entlang.

カアアワビーチ公園を散歩するハワイ女性。

Lovely Lumahai Beach on Kauai's north shore and (right) a cattle egret.

Hermosa playa de *Lumahai* — costa norteña de Kauai y (dcha.) garza de ganados.

La jolie plage *Lumahai Beach*, côte nord de Kaual et (à drolte) un Ibls.

Der wunderschöne Strand von *Lumahai Beach* an der Nordküste von Kauai und (rechts) Reiher.

カウアイ島北岸の美しいルマハイビーチと、（右）白さぎ。

Catching the waves off Sandy Beach, Oahu.   (right) Wave action at Pohakuloa Point, Molokai.

Cogiendo olas frente a *Sandy Beach*, Oahu.   (dcha.) Movimiento del oleaje en *Pohakuloa Point*, Molokai.

Rencontrant les vagues près de *Sandy Beach*, Oahu.   (à droite) Action des vagues à *Pohakuloa Point*, Molokai.

Wellenreiten vor *Sandy Beach* auf Oahu.   (rechts) Spiel der Wellen bei *Pohakuloa Point* auf Molokai.

オアフ島サンディービーチの波に乗って。　（右）　モロカイ島ポハク
ロア岬に砕ける波。

Palms reflected from a wind-rippled fishpond at Pu'uhonua o Honaunau, a national historical park on Hawaii's Kona Coast.   (right) A park employee demonstrates the lifestyle of his ancestors.

Palmeras reflejadas en un pozo en *Pu'uhonua o Honaunau*, parque histórico nacional en la costa de *Kona*.   (dcha.) Un empleado del parque revalida una habilidad de sus antepasados.

Le reflet des palmiers dans un étang plissé par le vent à *Pu'uhonua o Honaunau*, un parc national historique *Kona Coast*.   (à droite) Un jeune homme continue une tradition de ses ancêtres.

Bei *Pu'uhonua o Honaunau*, einem historischen Nationalpark auf der *Kona Coast* von Hawaii, spiegeln sich Palmen in einem windgekräuselten Fischteich.   (rechts) Ein Parkwächter führt den Lebensstil seiner Vorfahren vor.

水面に映るヤシの木。　ハワイ島コナ沿岸地プウホヌア・オ・ホナウナウの国立歴史公園の養魚池にて。

（左）　先祖伝来の生活を再現する公園職員。

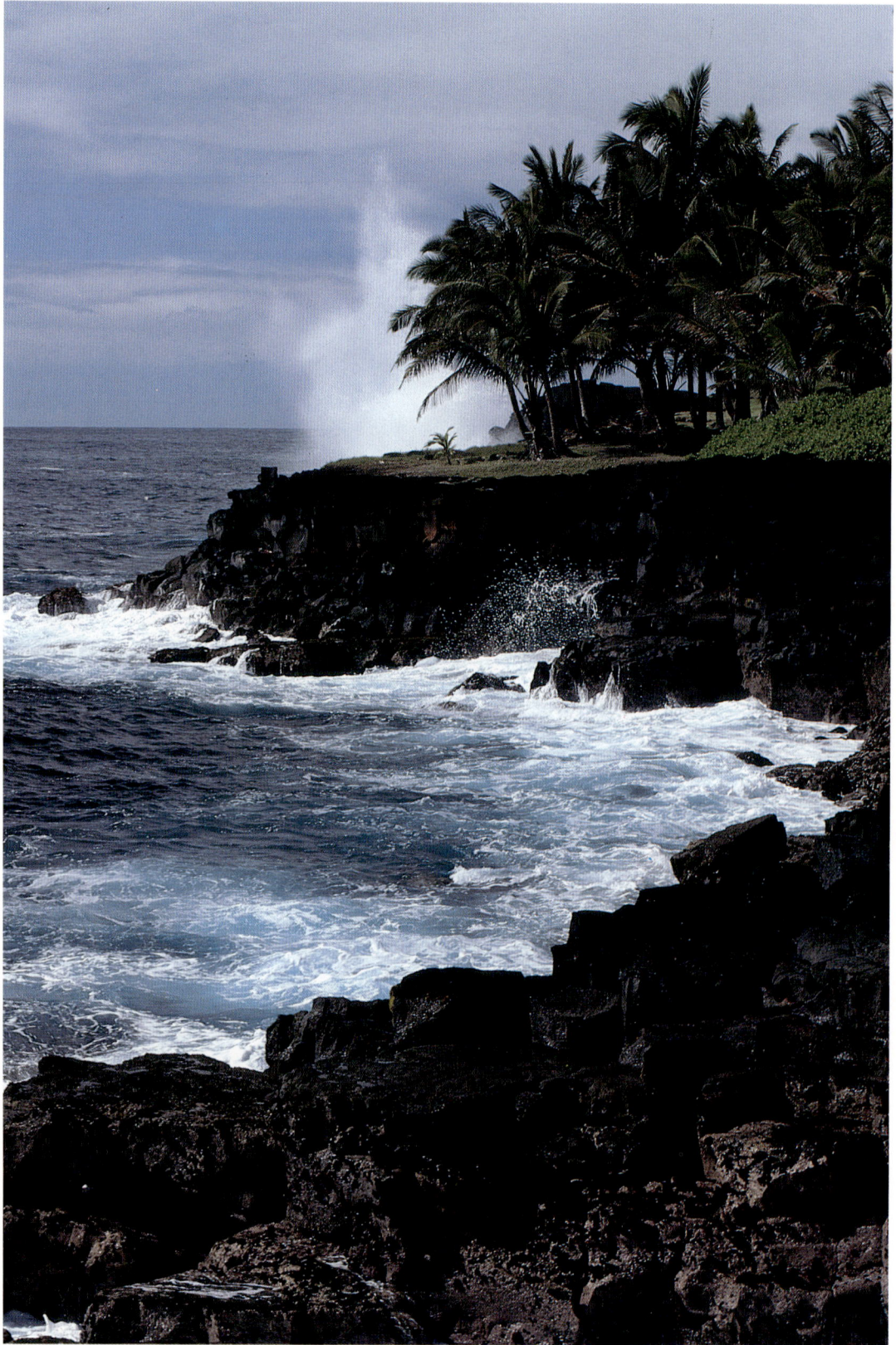

The wharf at Kaunakakai, Molokai rests on a placid morning sea.   (left) Rugged shoreline on The Big Island's Puna Coast.

El muelle de Kaunakakai, Molokai amanece sobre un mar tranquilo.   (izqda.) En la Isla Grande (Big Island) la escabrosa costa de *Puna*.

Le quai à Kaunakakai, Molokai se repose sur les eaux calmes du matin.   (à gauche) Côte escarpée de *Puna Coast*, The Big Island.

Die Landestelle von Kaunakakai auf Molokai steht ruhig im morgendlich friedlichen Meer.   (links) Rauhe Felsenküste an der *Puna Coast* der „Großen Insel".

静かな朝の海水にたゝずむモロカイ島カウナカカイふ頭。　（左）　ハワイ島プナ沿岸の荒々しい海岸線。

On West Maui resorts dot the water's edge as here at Kaanapali.   (right) Maui's popular, historic fishing village, Lahaina was once a home for Kamehameha the Great, king of Hawaii.

En West Maui, lugares de veraneo abundan al márgen del agua como aquí en Kaanapali.   (dcha.) El histórico pueblo pesquero de Lahaina, siempre popular, fue hogar de *Kamehameha El Grande*, rey de Hawaii.

La côte ouest de Maui est comblée de stations balnéaires comme celle-ci au bord des flots à Kaanapali.
(à droite) Le village de pèche historique, Lahina, où habitait autrefois le roi de Hawaii, *Kamehameha the Great*.

Auf West-Maui liegen am Meeresufer Seebäder verstreut, wie zum Beispiel hier Kaanapali.   (rechts) Lahaina, Mauis beliebter historischer Fischerort, war einst Wohnort des Königs von Hawaii, *Kamehameha the Great*.

マウイ島西岸カアナパリには、リゾート地が点在しています。　（右）　観光客に人気のあるマウイ島の旧い漁村ラハイナは、カメハメハ大王の主都でもありました。

The moon over a Maui cane burn.   (right) Death in lava's path, Hawaii Volcanoes National Park.

El plenilunio pende sobre la nocturna quemadura de caña de azúcar.   (dcha.) El río de lava trae la muerte en *Hawaii Volcanoes National Park*.

Maui sous la lune où on brule un champ de canne à sucre.   (à droite) La lave entraine la mort, *Hawaii Volcanoes National Park*.

Der Mond über einer Zuckerrohrverbrennung in Maui.   (rechts) Lava bringt Tod und Vernichtung, *Hawaii Volcanoes National Park*.

刈り入れ後のサトウキビ畑と月。　マウイ島。　（右）　溶岩に囲まれて。国立ハワイ火山公園にて。

At storm's break light finds its path to the Auau Channel off the Lanai coast and (left) Maui's Upcountry.

Rayos del sol penetran la tempestad menguante para iluminar el estrecho por la costa de Lanai y (izqda.) las alturas (*Upcountry*) de Maui.

Après la tempête, un rayon de lumière perce les nuages et rejoint le canal *Auau Channel* auprès de la côte de Lanai et (à gauche) les pays hauts, *Upcountry* de Maui.

Nach dem Unwetter bahnt sich das Licht einen Weg zum *Auau Channel* vor der Lanai-Küste, und (links) Mauis *Upcountry*.

近ずく嵐。　ラナイ島の沖、アウアウ海峡と、（左）　マウイ島の山岳地帯。

Ohia trees on a Na Pali Coast slope and (left) rich hues in Waimea Canyon, Kauai.

Arboles de ohia en un declive de la costa *Na Pali* y (izqda.) colores vivos en *Waimea Canyon*, Kauai.

Les arbres ohia sur une pente de la côte *Na Pali Coast* et (à gauche) vif coloris dans le cañon *Waimea Canyon*, Kauai.

Ohia-Bäume auf einem Abhang der *Na Pali Coast* und (links) satte Farbtöne im *Waimea Canyon* auf Kauai.

カウアイ島ナパリ沿岸のオヒアの木と、（左）　ワイメア・キャニオンの見事な色調。

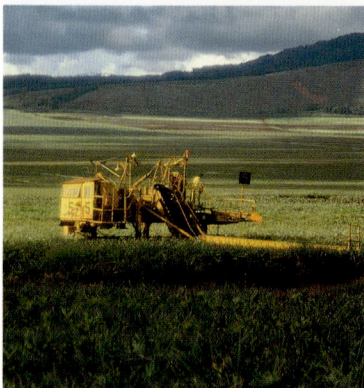

A bird's view of The Pineapple Island and (left) a harvest loading machine.

Vista aérea de The Pineapple Island (isla de Piñas) y (izqda.) aparato para cargar la cosecha.

Vue à vol d'oiseau, Pineapple Island (île aux ananas) et (à gauche) une machine à charger la récolte.

„The Pineapple Island" (Ananasinsel) aus der Vogelschau und (links) eine Maschine zum Einbringen der Ernte.

空からみたパイナップルの島と、（左）取入れ機。

Clouds curtain Lanai's Lanaihale.　(right) A wild orchid.

Nubes oscurecen *Lanaihale* en Lanai.　(dcha.) Una orquídea silvestre.

Les nuages enveloppent *Lanaihale*, Lanal.　(à droite) Une orchidée sauvage.

Wolken verhängen Lanais *Lanaihale*.　(rechts) Eine wilde Orchidee.

ラナイ島ラナイハレ山にかゝる雲。　（右）　野生ラン。

The Hanalei River and its lush fertile valley, Kauai.   (left) Elevated roadways on The Big Island's western slopes offer expansive views of the beautiful Kona Coast.

El *Río Hanalei* y su vega fértil, Kauai.   (izqda.) Caminos altos de los declives occidentales de la Isla Grande (Big Island) ofrecen vistas panorámicas de la hermosa *Kona Coast*.

La rivière *Hanalei* et sa vallée féconde, Kauai.   (à gauche) Telle que vue de ses routes élevées, la beauté de la côte occidentale de Kona s'épanouit à nos yeux.

Der *Hanalei River* und sein üppig fruchtbares Tal auf Kauai.   (links) Hochgebaute Straßen an den Westhängen der „Großen Insel" bieten einen weiten Blick auf die herrliche *Kona Coast*.

カウアイ島のハナレイ河と、肥沃な緑の谷。　（左）　ハワイ島西岸のスカイラインからは、コナ沿岸地帯が一望のもとに見渡せます。

From the four thousand foot level in Kokee State Park, Kauai, the eye is led across the verdant Kalalau Valley to the Na Pali Coast and a blue infinity.

Desde 1200 metros de altura en *Kokee State Park*, Kauai, la vista extiende a través del valle frondoso *Kalalau* hasta *Na Pali Coast* y más allá al azul infinito.

Vu de 1200 mètres de hauteur, le parc *Kokee State Park*, Kauai, dirige le regard à travers la vallée *Kalalau Valley* jusqu'à *Na Pali Coast* et vers l'infini.

Aus über 1200 m Höhe im *Kokee State Park* auf Kauai wandert der Blick über das frischgrüne Tal *Kalalau Valley* hinüber zur *Na Pali Coast* und in ein grenzenloses Blau.

カウアイ島コケエ州立公園の海抜４千フィートの地点から望む、緑のカララウ谷、ナパリ沿岸地帯と、はるかに浮ぶ太平洋。

Iao Valley gateway from the fringes of Wailuku and (left) Iao Needle, Maui.

La boca del *Iao Valley* vista desde las afueras de Wailuku y (izqda.) el pico, *Iao Needle* (Aguja de Iao), Maui.

L'entrée de la vallée *Iao Valley* vue de la lisière de Wailuku et (à gauche) *Iao Needle*, Maui.

Zugang zum Tal *Iao Valley* vom Stadtrand von Wailuku aus und (links) *Iao Needle*, Maui.

マウイ島ワイルクの町はずれよりみた、イアオ渓谷入り口と、　（左）　イアオ・ニードル。

Lichen-spattered trunks get a moment's attention from the sun, Hana District, Maui.   (right) Wailua Falls plunge over a canyon wall, Kauai.

Troncos pintados por líquenes gozan una caricia del sol en el distrito de Hana, Maui.   (dcha.) La catarata de *Wailua* se lanza al fondo de un cañón en Kauai.

Le soleil s'attarde sur l'écorce des arbres mouchetée de lichens, Hana District, Maui.   (à droite) Les chutes *Wailua Falls* franchissent le mur du ravin et y plongent.

Flechtenüberwachsene Baumstämme im Hana-Bezirk von Maui sind einen Augenblick lang von der Sonne beschienen.   (rechts) Das Gefälle der *Wailua Falls* auf Kauai stürzt über eine Canyon-Wand.

苔に飾られた木にもれる陽の光。　マウイ島ハナ地区にて。　（右）　岩壁落下するワイルア滝。　カウアイ島。

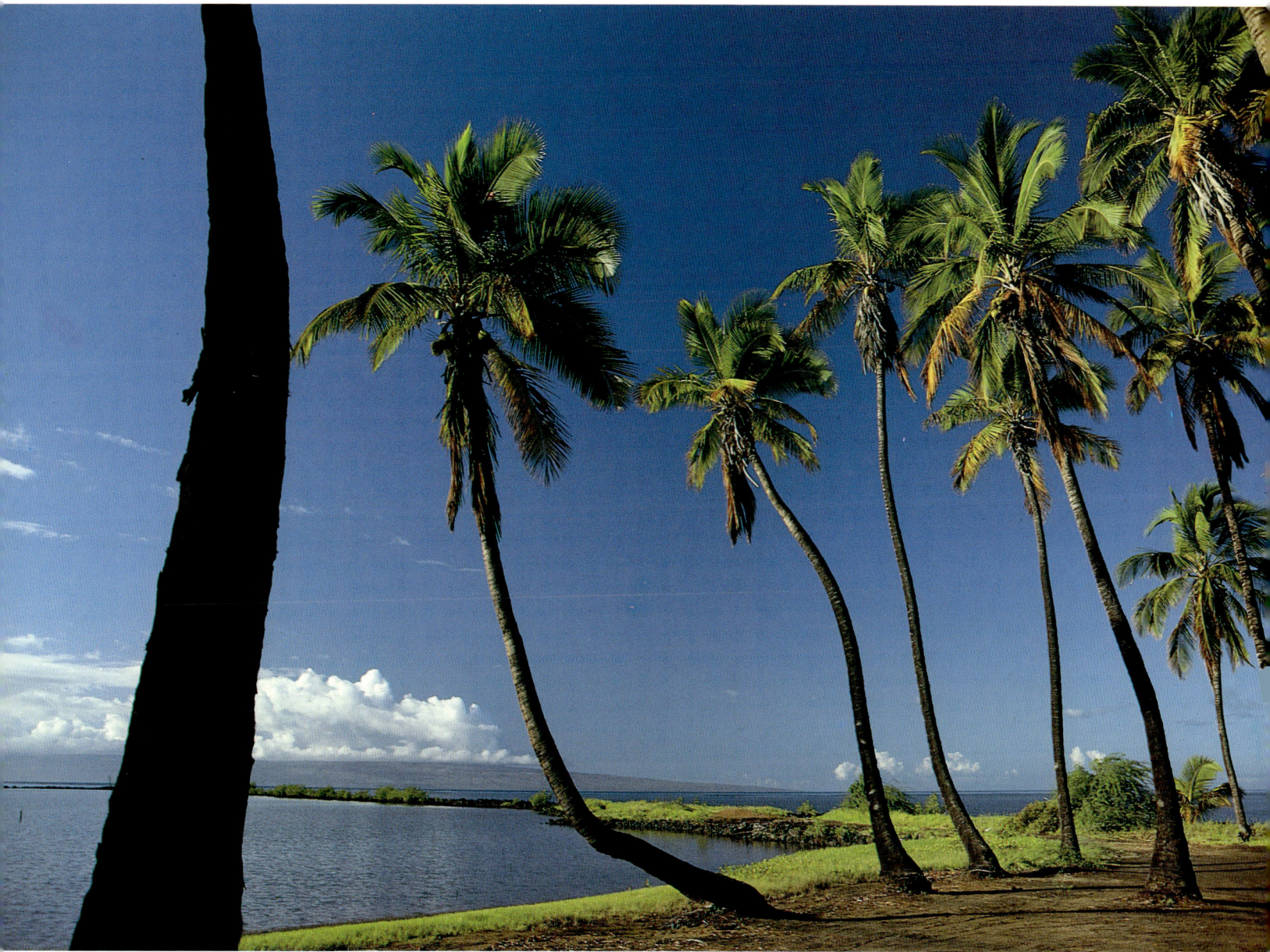

Graceful palms and an ancient fishpond once maintained to feed the ruling class create an idyllic setting on Molokai's southeast coast. (left) A coconut and low tide at Moku, Molokai.

Palmeras elegantes y un pozo antiguamente utilizado para mantener peces para nutrir a los aristócratas acentúan un idilio en la costa del suroeste de Molokai. (izqda.) Un coco espera la marea en la playa de Moku, Molokai.

Des palmiers gracieux et un vieil étang à poissons qui servait autrefois à nourrir la classe dirigeante, produisent une ambiance idyllique sur l'île Molokai. (à gauche) Un noix de coco à la marée basse à Moku, Molokai.

Anmutige Palmen und ein uralter Fischteich, der einstmals die herrschende Oberschicht versorgte, bieten diese idyllische Szene an der südöstlichen Küste von Molokai. (links) Eine Kokosnuß und Ebbe in Moku auf Molokai.

優雅なヤシの木々と、　かっての王族用養魚池は、このモロカイ島の東南沿岸部に、牧歌的なムードをたゞよわせています。(左)　ひき潮とヤシの実。　モロカイ島モクの海岸。

Maunas poke through a cloud cover over The Big Island.   (right) Frothy waves roll over rare black sand as a storm brews off the Puna Coast, Hawaii.

Maunas (montañas) dividen la cobija de nubes sobre *Big Island* (Isla Grande).   (dcha.) Olas espumosas inundan la arena negra que no es común, mientras una tormenta se hincha sobre *Puna Coast*, Hawaii.

Les *Maunas* couronnées de nuages parviennent à percer la nuée au delà de la grande île, The Big Island.   (à droite) La mer écumeuse, roule sur le sable noir pendant qu'au large de *Puna Coast*, Hawaii, un orage s'annonce.

Maunas durchstoßen die Wolkendecke über der „Großen Insel".   (rechts) Schaumwellen gleiten rasch über den ungewöhnlichen schwarzen Sand, während sich vor der *Puna Coast* von Hawaii ein Gewitter zusammenbraut.

たれこめる雲にそびえるマウナス山。　ハワイ島。　（右）　ハワイには珍しい黒い砂浜と、泡しぶき。　ハワイ島プナ海岸。

Warm, clean Hawaiian water laps at the shore of a small cove near Kanaha Point, Molokai.   (left) Lava stones snake their way out to sea, Kealia, Kauai.

El agua hawaiiana, limpia aunque no fría, lame en la playa de una pequeña ensenada cerca de *Kanaha Point*, Molokai. (izqda.) Las piedras de lava se insinúan al mar, Kealia, Kauai.

Les eaux hawaiiennes chaudes et claires, clapottent contre le rivage d'une petite baie peu profonde près de *Kanaha Point*, Molokai.   (à gauche) Des pierres formées de lave serpentent vers la mer, Kealia, Kauai.

Das warme, saubere Wasser von Hawaii spült an die Ufer einer kleinen Bucht bei *Kanaha Point* auf Molokai.   (links) In Kealia auf Kauai schlängelt sich Lavagestein auf dem Weg zum Meer.

温く透明なハワイの海。　モロカイ島カナハ岬の近くにて。　（左）　蛇行して海に届いた溶岩。　カウアイ島ケアリア。

Fun and sun beneath the palms at Hanauma Bay and (left) children fishing near Mokolii Island, Oahu.

Sol y sonrisa bajo las palmeras en la bahía de *Hanauma* y (izqda.) niños pescando cerca de la isla de *Mokolii*, Oahu.

Les beaux jours ensoleillés sous les palmiers à *Hanauma Bay* et (à gauche) les enfants font la pêche près de *Mokolii Island*, Oahu.

Sonnenschein und Frohsinn unter Palmen in der Bucht *Hanauma Bay* und (links) Kinder beim Fischfang nahe bei *Mokolii Island*, Oahu.

オアフ島。 太陽とヤシの木に色どられたハナウマ海岸と、 （左） モコリイ島近くで魚をつる子供達。

Honolulu's Ala Wai Canal and (left) Waikiki at dusk.

Ala Wai Canal, Honolulu y (izqda.) *Waikiki* al anochecer.

Ala Wai Canal, Honolulu, et (à gauche) *Waikiki* au crépuscule.

Der *Ala Wai Canal* von Honolulu und (links) *Waikiki* in der Abenddämmerung.

ホノルル市のアラワイ運河と、 （左） 夕ぐれのワイキキビーチ。

Sunning on Waikiki Beach. (right) A Japanese float entry in Honolulu's annual Aloha Week Floral Parade.

Tomando el sol en la playa de *Waikiki*. (dcha.) Una carroza japonesa en la procesión floral de *Aloha Week* (Semana de Aloha) de Honolulu.

Les bains de soleil sur la plage à *Waikiki Beach*. (à droite) Char japonais, un des participants du defilé de la parade de fleurs organisée tous les ans à Honolulu durant Aloha Week Floral Parade.

Sonnenbaden am *Waikiki Beach*. (rechts) Ein japanischer Beitrag zum alljährlichen Blumenfest in Honolulu während der Aloha-Woche.

ワイキキビーチで日光浴。（右）　年中行事アロハ・ウィーク・フローラル・パレードに参加する日本の山車。

Diamond Head, an extinct volcano and famous landmark as seen through masts in Ala Wai Harbor, Honolulu. (left) Canoeists paddle the city's waters.

Diamond Head (Cabo Diamante), un volcán extinguido, famosa atracción vista a través de los palos en el puerto *Ala Wai Harbor*, Honolulu. (izqda.) Las aguas de la ciudad lucen canoas.

Diamond Head, un volcan éteint, un point de repère bien connu, est visible entre les mats dans le port *Ala Wai Harbor*, Honolulu. (à gauche) Canoéistes pagayant leur barque dans les canaux de la région.

Diamond Head, ein untätiger Vulkan und berühmtes Wahrzeichen, durch Schiffsmaste im Hafen von Honolulu, *Ala Wai Harbor*, gesehen. (links) Paddler auf den Gewässern der Stadt.

ホノルル市アラワイ・ヨット・ハーバーよりみた、死火山ダイヤモンドヘッド。 （左） ホノルル市内にて。

Ohia and ferns, Hawaii Volcanoes National Park.   (left) Ancient trees reach for the sky at Kapuaiwa coconut grove on Molokai. Blossoms from left: lilikoi, false lehua, hau.

Ohia con helechos, *Hawaii Volcanoes National Park*.   (izqda.) Ancianos árboles se alzan al firmamento en el bosque de cocos llamado *Kapuaiwa* en Molokai. Flores, de izq. a dcha.: lilikoi, lehua falsa, hau.

Ohia et fougères, *Hawaii Volcanoes National Park*.   (à gauche) De très vieux arbres étendent leurs branches vers le ciel à *Kapuaiwa*, un bosquet de cocotiers à Molokai. Les fleurs de gauche à droite: lilikoi, fausse lehua, hau.

Ohia-Bäume und Farn im *Hawaii Volcanoes National Park*.   (links) Im Kokospalmenhain von *Kapuaiwa* auf Molokai strecken sich uralte Bäume himmelwärts. Die Namen der Blüten (von links nach rechts): lilikoi, falsche lehua, hau.

オヒアの木と羊歯。 （左） 国立ハワイ火山公園。 モロカイ島カプアイワ椰子園の天にも届くヤシの巨木。 左から順に、イリコイ、カリアンドラ、 ハウの花。

Kauai's legendary Alakoko Fishpond.   (right) Bringing home the lobster.

Alakoko Fishpond (Pozo de Peces de Alakoko) es legendario de Kauai.
(dcha.) Cosecha de langosta.

Un étang à poissons, sujet d'une légende *Alakoko Fishpond* sur l'île Kauai.   (à
droite) La récolte des fruits de mer.

Der sagenumwobene Fischteich *Alakoko Fishpond* auf Kauai.   (rechts) Der Hummer
wird eingebracht.

カウアイ島の伝説的なアラココ養魚池。　（右）　今日の糧。

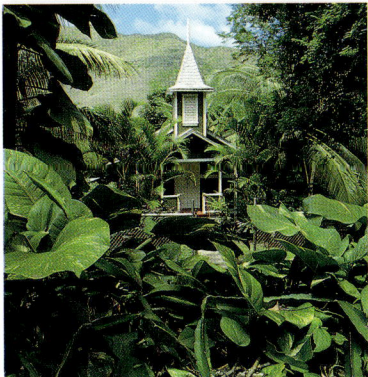

Sugar cane on Kauai.   (left) A small church, Halawa, Molokai.

Caña de azúcar en Kauai.   (izqda.) Una iglesia pequeña de Halawa, Molokai.

Canne a sucre sur l'île Kauai.   (à gauche) Une petite église, Halawa, Molokai.

Zuckerrohr auf Kauai.   (links) Eine kleine Kirche in Halawa auf Molokai.

サトウキビ畑。　カウアイ島。　（右）　モロカイ島ハラワの小教会。

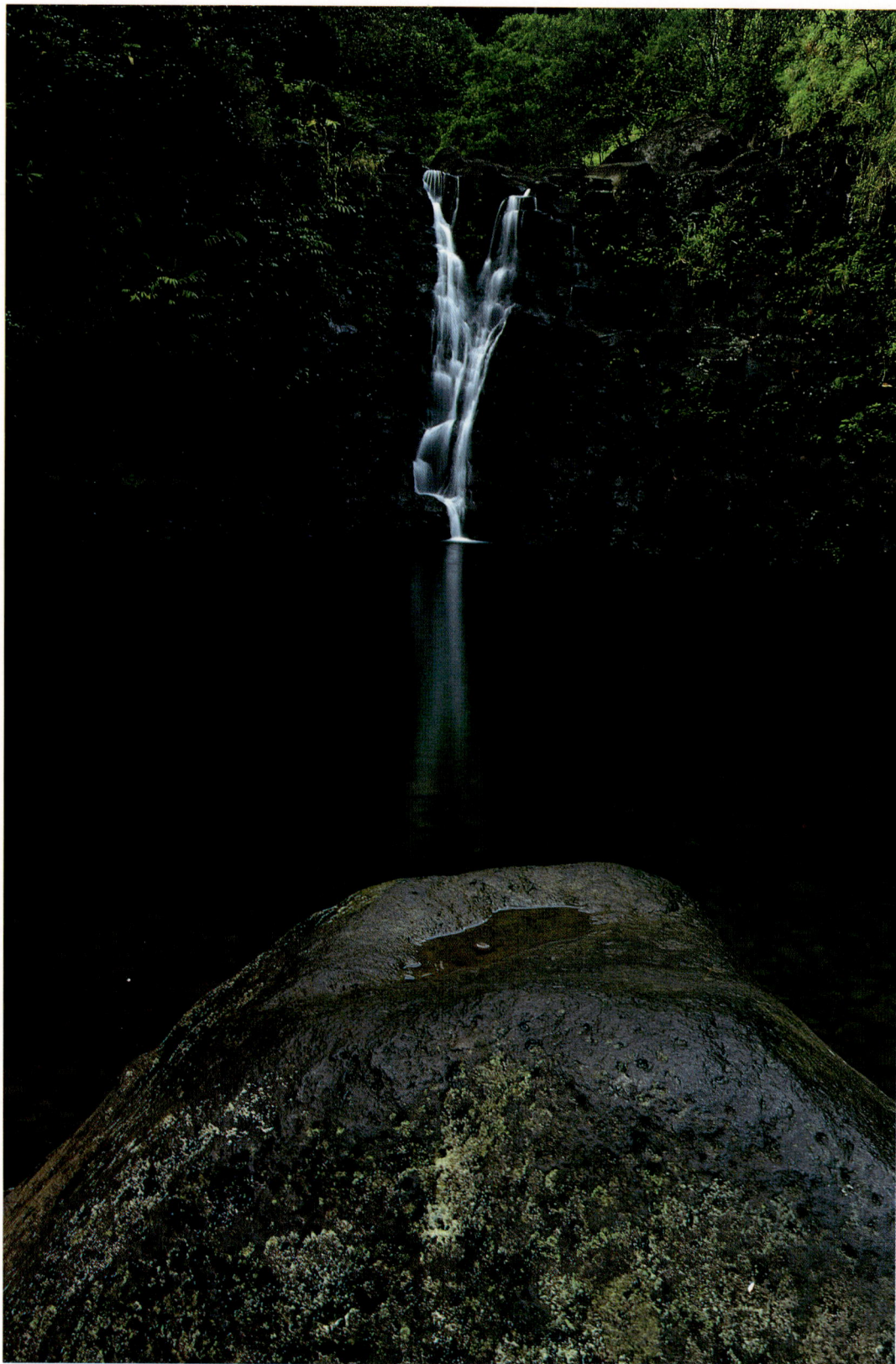

Varied trees and plants at Keanae Arboretum invite appreciative inspection, and (left) one of a myriad of waterfalls along the Hana Highway, Maui.

Arboles y plantas variadas de *Keanae Arboretum* invitan a grata atención y (izqda.) una de muchas cataratas a lo largo de *Hana Highway*, Maui.

Grande variété d'arbres et de plantes à *Keanae Arboretum* demandent une appréciation speciale et (à gauche) une des nombreuses chutes d'eau le long de *Hana Highway*, Maui.

Die verschiedensten Blumen und Pflanzen im *Keanae Arboretum* laden zum Anschauen und Bewundern ein, und (links) einer der unzähligen Wasserfälle am *Hana Highway* auf Maui.

マウイ島ケアナエ植物園の珍らしい木々と植物は、観賞者を誘います。 （左） マウイ島のハナ・ハイウェーぞいには、数多くの滝があります。

Kilauea's steamy Halemaumau Crater, Hawaii Volcanoes National Park. (right) Anthurium.

El cráter vaporoso, *Halemaumau Crater, Hawaii Volcanoes National Park*, Kilauea. (dcha.) Anthurium.

La vapeur s'échappe du cratère sur Kilauea, *Halemaumau Crater, Hawaii Volcanoes National Park*. (à droite) Anthurium.

Der dampfende Krater Kilaueas, *Halemaumau Crater,* im *Hawaii Volcanoes National Park*. (rechts) Anthurium.

キラウェア火山の、ハレマウマウ噴火口。 国立ハワイ火山公園。 （右） アンセリュームの花。

Inside Haleakala Crater and (left) Science City, Maui. (overleaf) A Maui sunset.

Dentro de *Haleakala Crater* y (izqda.) Science City (Ciudad de Ciencias), Maui. (pag. siguiente:) Puesta del sol en Maui.

L'intérieur du cratère *Haleakala Crater* et (à gauche) Science City, Maui. Un coucher du soleil à Maui.

Im Innern des *Haleakala Crater* und (links) Science City, Maui. (umseitig) Sonnenuntergang auf Maui.

マウイ島ハレアカラ噴火口内部と、 （左） サイエンス・シティー。 （離面） マウイの夕陽。

Koa on Molokai.   (right) The flower of an African Tulip Tree.   (left) A colorful slice of Waimea Canyon, Kauai.

Koa de Molokai.   (dcha.) La flor de un tulípero africano.   (izqda.) Un trozo colorido de *Waimea Canyon*, Kauai.

Les arbres Koa sur Molokai.   (à droite) La fleur d'un tulipier africain African Tulip Tree.   (à gauche) La nature colore une tranche du cañon *Waimea Canyon*, Kauai.

Koa-Bäume auf Molokai.   (rechts) Blüte eines afrikanischen Tulpenbaumes.   (links) Ein bunter Ausschnitt des *Waimea Canyon* auf Kauai.

コアの木。　モロカイ島。　（右）　アフリカ・チューリップの花。　カウアイ島 ワイメアキャニオン。

A paradise cove at Waikoko Bay, Kauai. (right) Winds, treacherous water currents and a reef lined north shore on Lanai help give rise to the name of Shipwreck Beach.

Una ensenada paradisíaca en la bahía, *Waikoko Bay*, Kauai. (dcha.) Viento, corrientes traidores y una costa norteña llena de arrecifes han conferido el nombre *Shipwreck Beach* (Playa de Naufragios) a esta parte de Lanai.

Un coin du paradis à *Waikoko Bay*, Kauai. (à droite) Dû aux vents, aux eaux traitresses et au récif de corail qui longe la rive nord de Lanai, de nombreux navires ont fait naufrage sur cette plage qu'on applelle *Shipwreck Beach*.

Eine paradiesische Bucht in der *Waikoko Bay* auf Kauai. (rechts) Wind, gefährliche Wasserströmungen und Felsenklippen haben der Nordküste von Lanai den Namen *Shipwreck Beach* eingebracht.

カウアイ島ワイココ湾にて。 （右） 吹きすさぶ風と危険な海流、辺りをとりまく珊瑚礁をみれば、ラナイ島北岸の難破船海岸という名の由来も分ります。

Early morning waves line up to impact a lava outcropping near Ahihi Point, Kauai. (right) Water swirls around days last glint of light cast on lava stones near the base of Kaholo Pali, Lanai.

Las olas de la madrugada hacen cola para aplastarse contra un cabo de lava cerca de *Ahihi Point*, Kauai. (dcha.) El agua circula alrededor del último rayo de luz reflejado por piedras de lava cerca de la base de *Kaholo Pali*, Lanai.

Au petit matin, les vagues s'alignent prêtes à se précipiter sur un affleurement de lave près de *Ahihi Point*, Kauai. (à droite) Refoulement d'eau au contact des pierres de lave éclairées par la dernière lueur du jour à la base de *Kaholo Pali*, Lanai.

Früh am Morgen wappnen sich die Wellen gegen den Lavaausfluß bei *Ahihi Point* auf Kauai. (rechts) Im letzten Licht des Tages wirft das Wasser seine Kreise um das Lavagestein am Fuße des *Kaholo Pali* auf Lanai.

溶岩に当りくだける順番を待つ波頭。　カウアイ島アヒヒ岬の近くにて。　（右）　渦まく波。　ラナイ島カホロパリ。

Maui's Upcountry in the shadow of mighty Haleakala Crater.
(right) Atop a young silversword plant.

Upcountry (alturas) de Maui en la sombra del formidable *Haleakala Crater*. (dcha.) Encima de un ejemplar joven de la planta llamada Silversword (Espada de plata).

Les pays hauts de Maui *(Upcountry)* dans l'ombre du puissant cratère *Haleakala Crater*. (à droite) Vue du haut, une jeune plante silversword.

Mauis *Upcountry* im Schatten des mächtigen *Haleakala Crater*. (rechts) Auf der Spitze einer jungen Silberschwertpflanze.

雄大なハレアカラ噴火口足元のマウイ島山岳地帯。 （右） 若いシルバーウッドの木を真上からみる。

Stately ohia trees near Lanai City and (left) bamboo.

El ohia es un árbol elegante que abunda cerca de Lanai City y también (izqda.) el bambú.

Les ohia majestueux près de Lanai City et (à gauche) du bambou.

Stattliche Ohia-Bäume bei Lanai City und (links) Bambus.

見事なオヒアの木と、（左）竹。　ラナイ市附近。

A discharge from heaven's storehouse into the Kealaikahiki Channel off Palaoa Point, Lanai.   (right) Evening respite for the popular sands of Ke'e Beach, Kauai.

Una descarga del almacén del cielo llega al estrecho *Kealaikahiki Channel* por *Palaoa Point*, Lanai.   (dcha.) Sosiego crepuscular para las arenas populares de *Ke'e Beach,* Kauai.

Se déchargent des nuages, l'entrepôt du ciel, le pluis gonflent le canal *Kealaikahiki Channel* au large de *Palaoa Point*, Lanai.   (à droite) Le soir apporte un temps de répit à la plage sabloneuse qui, durant le jour, jouit d'une grande popularité auprès des baigneurs, *Ke'e Beach,* Kauai.

Der Himmel entlädt sich in den *Kealaikahiki Channel* vor *Palaoa Point* auf Lanai.   (rechts) Abendruhe für den beliebten Sandstrand von *Ke'e Beach,* auf Kauai.

パラオア岬の雨。　ラナイ島。　（右）ケエビーチの夕ぐれ。　カウアイ島。

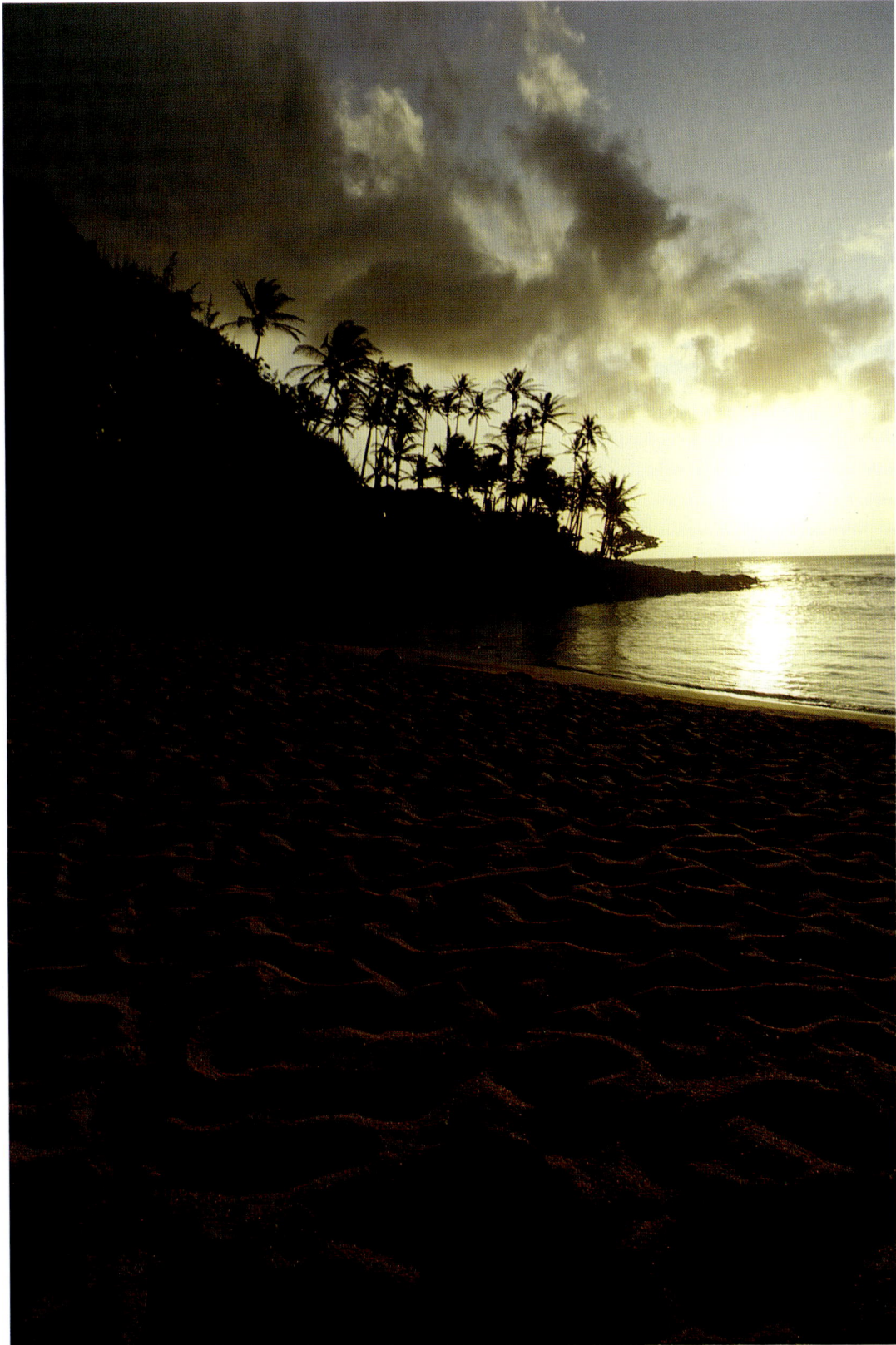

U.S. Geological Survey photos by J. D. Griggs and (below) George Ellrich

Molten lava spews forth from the *East Rift* of *Kilauea*, Hawaii.

Lava fundida surge de *East Rift* (Grieta del Este), *Kilauea*, Hawaii.

Les laves vomies par le volcan *East Rift* de *Kilauea*, Hawaii.

Flüssige Lava quillt aus dem *East Rift* des *Kilauea* auf Hawaii.

キラウェア火山 「イースト・リフト」から、吹き出す蒸気。　ハワイ島。